city sports

English translation © Copyright 1992 by Barron's Educational Series, Inc.

© Parramón Ediciones, S.A.
Published by Parramón Ediciones, S.A., Barcelona, Spain
The title of the Spanish edition is *Los deportes en la ciudad.*
Author: Isidro Sánchez; illustrator: Carme Peris; translated from the
Spanish by Edith Wilson

All inquiries should be addressed to:
Barron's Educational Series, Inc.
250 Wireless Boulevard
Hauppauge, New York 11788

Library of Congress Catalog Card No. 91-32928

International Standard Book No. 0-8120-4866-0

Library of Congress Cataloging-in-Publication Data
Sánchez, Isidro.
    [Deportes en la cuidad.   English]
    City sports / Isidro Sánchez, Carme Peris ; [translated from the Spanish
by Edith Wilson].
        p.   cm. — (The World of sports)
    Translation of: Los deportes en la ciudad.
    Summary: Briefly describes some of the sports that can be enjoyed in
urban areas, such as running. tennis, soccer, basketball, and gymnastics.
    ISBN 0-8120-4866-0
    1. Sports—Juvenile literature. [1. Sports.   2. City and town life.]
I. Peris, Carme, ill.   II. Title.   II. Series: Sánchez, Isidro.
World of sports.
GV706.8.S2513   1992
796—dc20   91-32928
                                                        CIP
                                                        AC

Printed in Spain
2345   0987654321

the world of sports

city sports

Isidro Sánchez
Carme Peris

BARRON'S

In the city there are parks and playgrounds where we can run and play safely—away from cars, trucks, and crowds of people.

A marathon is run every year in our city. Adults and older children can join in the race. To some people winning is not the most important thing—they just want to be a part of it!

It is exciting to watch Mom play tennis.
She trains long and hard, so she has
become a good player.

Teamwork is very important in soccer. To play well and score goals, we must all work together.

Gymnasts need to have a flexible body and a good sense of rhythm. They must also have strength to perform on the rings, the balance beam, the horse, and the parallel bars.

In judo class we learn the art of self-defense. We also learn how to practice without harming our "opponent."

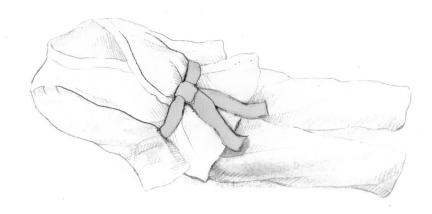

Basketball is very fast and very exciting.
The players must keep running and
passing the ball. Whoever is close
enough tries to shoot it into the basket.

Dad explains the rules of volleyball to us. The players must hit the ball with both hands to get it over the net. They must not let the ball touch the ground.

Football is a rough and exciting sport. The players throw the ball and carry it across the field, dodging the tackles of their opponents.

In our city there are wading pools for us to splash in and Olympic-sized pools for swimming competitions.

I already know how to do the butterfly stroke!

To win the 100-yard dash, the runners must be very fast getting out of the blocks at the start of the race.

This is a hurdle race. It looks very difficult. These athletes not only have to run very fast—they must also jump over the high hurdles that have been placed in the track!

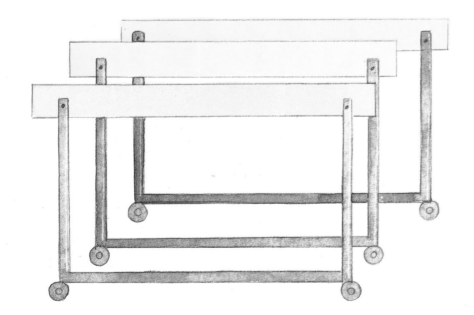

Later, Dad takes us to see the jumping and throwing competitions. Each of these athletes has trained very hard and wants to break the record.

CITY SPORTS

Sports—An Urban Phenomenon

With the exception of sports that can only occur in a particular natural environment (for example, skiing, mountaineering, sailing, etc.), most sports require sites that are available in an urban setting.

Spectator sports are an urban phenomenon.

Setting Records

Track and field competition includes a variety of activities designed to test three basic athletic skills: running, jumping, and throwing.

Running events consist of flat and hurdle races of varying lengths. There are short dashes —100 yards, 100 meters, and 200 meters; intermediate runs—400 meters and 800 meters; and long-distance runs—1 mile, 1,500 meters and 10,000 meters. Walking (distances may reach over 12 miles) and marathon races (with distances of over 26 miles) are among the longest events.

In relay races teams of four runners compete against each other. A baton that is carried by the first runner must be passed from one team member to the next throughout the race. Olympic relay races consist of the 4 x 110, 400, and 3,000 meter races.

Jumping events include the long jump, triple jump, high jump, and pole vault.

In the long jump, an athlete runs along the track to a point behind the scratch line. Then the jumper leaps on one foot without touching the ground beyond the takeoff point. While in the air, the jumper can propel him- or herself farther by thrusting and stretching the body and limbs. The jump is measured from the scratch line to the nearest imprint made by the competitor on the sand of the landing area.

In the triple jump, the first leap is made from one foot, and that same foot must be used in landing. The jump continues with the competitor taking a long step to the other foot, then leaping into the final jump from which he or she must land with both feet on the sand.

The high jump requires a contestant to clear a horizontal bar, the height of which is progressively increased. At each height, the athlete is given three chances to clear the bar without knocking it down.

The pole used for vaulting may be over 16 feet (5 m) long. It is balanced in the hands during the run. Takeoff in vaulting must be made by placing the pole in the takeoff box. A fast running speed helps the athlete execute the jump and balance the pole. The bending of the pole during takeoff provides the force necessary to clear the crossbar.

Throwing events make use of the following devices: javelin, discus, hammer, shot, and heavy weight. The javelin is a spear-like shaft; the discus is a thick disk; the hammer, shot, and heavy weight are all spheres.

Ancient Combat

An early form of unarmed self-defense developed by Tibetan monks has given rise to the modern Oriental systems of defense. In 1882 Jigoro Kano, a Japanese student of jujitsu, developed his own self-defense system, called ju-do, and founded the first judo school.

Combatants are ranked by skill and awarded belts of different colors, according to their classification. In addition to the black belt—the highest judo classification reserved for experts—there are other belt colors denoting different degrees of skill. These include brown, which ranks just below black; and white, which is given to beginners.

A Sport for Giants

In 1891 James Naismith, an instructor at the International YMCA Training School (now Springfield College), in Springfield, Massachusetts, developed the rules for a game that could be played in the confines of the school gym. He named it "basketball," because peach baskets were initially used as goals.

Basketball soon gained such popularity that the rules and technical aspects of the game evolved at a furious pace. In 1904 the Olympics featured a basketball demonstration tournament, but it was not until the Berlin Olympics of 1936 that basketball became an Olympic sport.

Ball in the Air

Volleyball was also created by a physical education teacher, William G. Morgan, in

Massachusetts. In 1949 the first world championships were held. Volleyball has been an Olympic sport since 1952.

The game consists of passing the ball across a net to the other side, hitting it with both hands or any other part of the body above the waist. No player on the team may touch the ball two consecutive times; nor may a team touch the ball more than three times in returning it to the other side of the net.

Sports and the Child

Sports activities are increasingly available to all people. Therefore, it is not surprising to find young children who are tantalized by the opportunities offered to them in school and elsewhere.

Nevertheless, as experts in physical education warn, not all sports are appropriate for a young child. Lifting and throwing weights, for example, is not recommended before adolescence. On the other hand, rhythmic gymnastic maneuvers and swimming are regarded as appropriate exercise at an early age.

Read and Think Questions for Children

1. This book tells about many different sports. Which one do you think you would most enjoy doing? Which sport would you most enjoy watching? Why?

2. In which sports is it important that you work as a team? In which do you work more by yourself? Find pictures of each type of sport in your book.

3. Look at the picture of the gymnasts performing. What kinds of skills must gymnasts have? Which sort of gymnast would you most like to be?

4. Volleyball, basketball, soccer, and football are all sports that use balls. How are these sports alike? How are they different?

5. What are some good reasons for wanting to play sports?